DESKTOP DIGITAL VIDEO PRODUCTION

ISBN 0-13-795600-2

90000

9 780137 956005

Prentice Hall IMSC Press Multimedia Series
Bing Sheu, *Series Editor*

▶ **Desktop Digital Video Production**
Frederic Jones